Sh

Untitled, Unfiltered, and Unleashed.

With love

♡ always,
Kylee Carlson

Kylee K. Carlson

Sheila –

With love

♡ Mommy,
 Judy & Harry

These words are for you Dad.

My rock.

My inspiration.

You lead me to write and didn't know this would become my healing.

I love you.

Contents

Unorganized.

You broke me into tiny pieces making me believe that was what I deserved.

Destroying the way I thought about myself.

Slowly changing who I was to fit into the mold you wanted.

Harsh words spilled from your mouth,

                    Leaving tiny bruises covering my heart.

Darker than the bruises you left on my skin.

New password.

Hidden texts.

Deleted pictures.

Change in your attitude.

Letting me imagine I wasn't enough.

-I was not the problem.

We once ignited like a firework.

Exploding with beauty for all to see.

But that's what we were.

A show for everyone to watch on the fourth of July.

Don't forget that fireworks fizzle out faster than they fill the night sky.

The Doctors words shred all my dreams I created for my future.

My greatest fear came true.

Until I came home to you.

Relief covered your face as tears streamed mine.

The one thing I wanted to become was never going to be.

And through my heartbreak you weren't there for me.

Spending days glued to my bed too sad to move.

Not once did your face appear at my door asking if I was okay.

And I was not, at least not today.

My body is my castle.

Heart kept locked in the dungeon

Mind kept locked in the tower

Mind tells lies to Heart

For Heart believes in happy endings

But Mind knows not to believe such fairy tales.

All my anger building to the edge.

Asking me to do things for you

Things you don't do for me.

Finally, I grew the courage to talk.

But you were drunk

And that was never a good time.

No matter how much love you give a toxic person they are still poisoning the air that fills your lungs.

Slowly killing your hopes

And your happiness.

The way you disappeared from your eyes haunts me.

I watched as anger took over and pushed you aside.

Your pupils dilated, covering your beautiful hazel eyes.

Fists clenched at your sides.

Sweat building above your lip.

Attempting to run to the bedroom was a bad idea.

I still wake from my dreams gasping for breath

As your hands around my throat scar my mind

And the sting of your hand burns my skin.

You pushed.

I pulled.

You ran.

I chased.

Like a puppy I followed you.

No matter how deeply you hurt me.

The words that fell from your lips

Still echoing in my head.

You never felt you were in the wrong

Making me believe I kept messing up.

Until finally

You pushed.

I pushed back.

Living together.

Every day.

Every night.

Together.

Never felt so alone.

Touching. Kissing. Fucking. Taking.

Always what you wanted.

Never what I needed.

Hurting. Bruising. Apologizing.

One day I had to realize I couldn't hold on to our happy memories forever.

The laughs we shared.

The day at the beach.

The soccer games.

The road trips.

But after you started to mess with my head I started to replace the good with the bad.

The tears I shed.

The times I went to sleep alone.

The times I caught you cheating.

The times you got physical.

The embarrassment you made me feel.

All replaced by resentment.

Your words sliced through my skin.

First, they felt like papercuts.

Then they grew to burns that bubbled and blistered.

Leaving scars that only my eyes could see.

My body hurts for what is no longer there.

My heart craves to love someone who does not exist.

My mind is restless.

I am weak.

-I will be stronger tomorrow.

You are the first thing I think of every morning.

But is that because you are the cause of my pain or my happiness?

You were like a drug.

As soon as you hit my bloodstream the high took over.

Pure ecstasy.

We couldn't get enough of each other.

Until one of us got addicted

While the other was always looking for the next high.

You couldn't handle the comedown

I'm thankful to be sober.

Our love burned like a flame.

Beautiful to the naked eye

Yet harmful to anyone who stands too close.

I was the fuel

You were the spark.

Together we ignite.

Eventually one fades

And the fire goes out.

Your touch drove me wild

Sparking something inside me I didn't know was there.

I craved your fingers as soon as they left my skin.

Always wanting more.

Only you never gave me what I needed.

Leaving me alone in our bed for hours.

Waiting.

Then you stopped touching me at all.

When you finally touched me again

Your touch made me sick.

Never wanting such poison to graze me

Ever again.

You liked my hair when it was long enough to tickle my hips,

I cut it off.

You liked my body because I was fit and skinny,

I gained 15 pounds.

You liked it when I got high with you,

I quit.

-I did it all for me.

"You have lost your sparkle." She said.

Her words snapped me back to reality.

My sparkle was who I was

How could I have lost her?

For myself,

I will find my sparkle.

So, I left.

Friends disappeared

Along with everything you owned.

Half of the closet empty.

Your stupid flag,

Everything you was

Gone.

For the first time in a long time

I could breathe.

Taking care of only myself was foreign to me

I didn't know how to just be.

Putting everyone above myself

No longer was I going to sit on a shelf.

One step at a time

I start to make the climb.

She loved everyone around her so deeply

But somewhere between being used and taken for granted

She got lost and hurt.

She didn't have enough love left for the one that mattered most

    Herself.

Why doesn't it hurt as much as I expected?

You are gone

and I feel fine.

Do not even feel lonely.

I guess I went through the breakup

Before we even broke up.

Lost in a maze with only dead ends.

Every turn I make is the wrong one.

The walls begin to grow around me

Cutting off the sunlight that sets upon my skin

And the oxygen that fills my lungs.

Allowing the maze to consume everything I am.

The vines biting into my skin

Stealing all my strength.

Weakness taking over my body.

Slowly allowing the walls to swallow me whole.

Closing my eyes as the darkness surrounds me

Something shoots light into my heart

Not love.

Not him.

Me.

Hope in myself.

I am important.

Slowly the vines loosen their grip

Letting the light back in.

And I rise to my feet

To find my way out of this maze.

"You're good enough you know." He said.

But he still left.

Forgive.

But I never forgot.

Hurt.

But I grew stronger.

Sadness.

But now I smile.

And that's because of me.

It took getting hurt

Over

And over again

by the same man

To realize

I did need him in my life,

But not the way I had thought.

I needed him to find myself again.

To push me onto a different path.

His harsh words still echo in my head

But now I use them to push myself.

Reminding myself how far I have grown.

Plain white walls.

Blank.

Plain white furniture.

Empty.

This is our home

Quiet.

We built together.

Lonely.

When you left

I painted the walls pink.

-this is my house now.

The truth spills out

No matter how much you deny it.

Making yourself look worse,

With each lie that falls from your lips.

Don't forget we always find out the truth.

Music saved me.

She sent vibrations through my body restarting my heart.

Wrapping her words around me,

She holds me.

When I couldn't get out of bed

Music was my shoulder to lean on.

Not once has she left my side.

Her energy is contagious

Letting her take control of my body.

Music saved me.

Suicide.

Passes through my thoughts

Like the beautiful woman at the bar

You were too scared to talk to.

From a distance, you admire her

But you know her dating history

And that woman is trouble.

So, you leave the bar.

I am suicidal.

But I would never end my life.

Leaving behind everything would not solve the pain

Just pass the pain along to the next victim.

Loneliness is a good friend of mine.

He used to make me fear the dark.

Consuming me.

Sparking my anxiety.

But after spending all my days and nights

With Loneliness by my side

We now hold hands.

He has taught me how to love myself more.

He makes me tell myself I am beautiful.

Loneliness became inviting.

But eventually,

Loneliness leaves too.

A letter to you.

I don't remember you being in my life. I didn't really know you until I was an adult and learned for myself. You have nothing to do with me. Not once have I ever felt like a mistake but that's probably because you were never there to make me feel like one. So, what I am trying to say is, thank you. Thank you for creating me and leaving. Thank you for stepping aside so someone else could raise me as their own. Thank you for not being there. Why am I thanking you? Well if you didn't I would not have the amazing dad in my life that I have now. He stepped up when he didn't have to. He raised me to be the kind, bold, weird, funny, stubborn woman I am today. He is there for me when I am a mess and need a shoulder to cry on. He makes promises he keeps. He gave me two of my very best friends. I would not be the strong woman I am today if you had stayed. i have no idea how different my life would be if you were in it but I have grown to be thankful for the people who have stuck around because they care for me and want to be a part of my story. I am not mad, I am thankful.

She is back.

The beautiful girl from the bar.

She looks different this time.

Brighter. Happier.

She is looking at me.

Smiling.

I really want to dance with her.

Buy her a drink.

Maybe I will this time.

I am a lotus flower.

No matter how dirty and murky my pond may be around me,

I will grow to be beautiful.

Rising above the dirty water.

There she stands.

The girl at the bar.

We danced.

The way we moved felt intoxicating.

I let her consume me for the night.

When it was time to go home she wouldn't take me with her.

I woke up alone in my bed

Craving to get a little bit closer to her.

Empty.

Hollow.

Vacant.

Life flows all around me but I am numb.

Standing in line at a coffee shop I hear the words speak from someone's phone

"it is okay not to be okay."

And I could have sworn I felt my heartbeat again.

But this time it beat for me.

Letter to me.

      Stop being so fucking sad. You need to stop feeling sorry for yourself and stop crying all the time. The most important part is you finally opened your heart and loved again. You told your deepest darkest secrets you have never even said out loud. You did everything you could but you cannot fix the broken. Just please stop crying.

Today I am broken.

I cracked.

My chest aches.

The tears won't stop falling.

You were the person I finally saw a future with.

Someone I didn't have to fix.

I didn't see it coming.

Now I lay here

Empty

My heart beat only for you

Now I can't feel it at all

As it still lies in your hands.

Her heart slowly started to grow thorns.

Stabbing anyone who gets too close.

My inner bitch has taken over my body.

The sweetheart everyone has come to know and love

Is gone.

I have no filter.

My inner bitch likes to speak what pops

Into her mind.

She only should worry about herself

Doesn't give a damn what other people think.

Weight has fallen from my bones.

My appetite has disintegrated

Along with the little curves I had.

Depression eats away at everything I am.

First, he ate my mind.

Then he took my strength.

Watching me as I lay lifeless in my bed.

Slowly sinking away.

Last, he tried to take my soul,

But that just would not do.

I needed to feel actual pain.

Something other than heartache

And numbness.

So, I got a tattoo.

When the brainwashing finally ends

The world feels different.

Anxiety hovering over my shoulder with every step I take.

The echo of his voice was silenced.

Only my thoughts.

My dreams.

Finally, in a world of my own.

She walks into my workplace this time.

Somehow, she looks more beautiful.

Her eyes locking mine as she walks over to me.

Something doesn't feel right this time.

I do not want her here.

Yet here she is sliding her way back into my life.

Wanting me to join her.

Pulling on my hand towards the door.

No.

Not this time.

Love is like a drug they said.

Never understood what that meant

Until I tasted its bitterness on my tongue.

But once I let the high take over

Loves beauty was undeniable.

Making my heart race and my palms sweat.

Love was everywhere.

After time Love fades away like all drugs do,

And the comedown hurts like hell.

Never wanting to feel the pain of heartbreak again.

Not allowing yourself to become an addict.

But you crave the Love of another.

I am not a doormat.

You do not get to wipe your dirty shoes across me

Ignoring that I am there at all.

I am a person

With feelings and a voice.

My depression is like a ghost.

Always lurking and watching my every move.

Riding around on my shoulders

Exhausting me to the core.

My depression likes to possess me.

Overriding my brains software.

Leaving me a helpless memory.

I thought I would be okay.

I was used to people leaving.

They always do.

But you are different.

You cared.

You gave me a voice when I thought I lost it.

Around you I felt safe and

For the first time

I felt loved.

But you broke me.

You left.

You were the hammer

I was the nail

Making me smaller

And smaller

with each blow.

Cheating is a choice.

Loneliness will tempt you.

Pain will push you.

Love will hide in your mind.

But the choice is yours

Rise above or

Kill two people with one bullet.

I am not incomplete.

I am not untouched.

But I am unfinished.

Be patient you said.

I waited.

And waited.

Eventually I gave up.

Then you decided to care.

Sadness doesn't hang around as much as she used to.

She nestled into my home as if it were her own.

Taking up too much space.

That bitch didn't pay rent so

It was time to leave.

Suicide is a real tease.

Always making you think she is what's best for you.

Pushing you to believe.

Hiding the truth behind her back.

She is toxic.

But she does look intoxicating from time to time.

Until I see her claim her next victim.

Leaving you taught me I was important.

Growing away from you

Pushed me to fall in love with me.

I never thought I could be so madly in love with

Me.

She cannot be weakened by the small minds of others.

When was the last time you said "I love you"

To yourself?

Today I woke up and I missed you.

Rolling over to find you not beside me.

The pain struck me for a while as I just lay there thinking of your snores.

The way they roared from your mouth.

I missed listening to you while you kept sleeping because I was an early bird and you were always the sleepy bear.

My heart ached but now my heart is healing.

No longer being angry at myself for falling in love with you.

Only feeling thankful.

For you found me in my darkness and taught me to love again.

Even when you couldn't hold the weight of our relationship.

I forgave you, but I think I will always have a piece of me that misses

What we shared.

Depression can consume and destroy one's mind.

It was up to me to rise again

And I was going to rise higher

Than anyone thought possible.

Self-love is hard to find

When you are just the

Awkward girl with a pretty face.

No one sees you as the

Bright energetic person you truly are.

Hiding away in your shell.

Until one day you let yourself free.

Free from the thoughts of others

Free to let yourself see

Who you are.

Spreading your light.

What you think of yourself

Matters most.

Women take breakups harder than men because we know how amazing we are. We know our worth. Women also see the future we built in our minds with our significant other. The house we would share. The dogs we would take for walks every morning. Our beautiful wedding day that we would share with our families. The adventures we would go on to see the world together. Our beautiful babies we would bring into the world and teach to play soccer and baseball. Raising them to be the best people they could possibly be. Together we would grow old. With each other. Breakups ruin all of that because we see your potential. Women see all. Once the significant other is out of the picture we must try to erase all the happy beautiful moments we shared together and the moments we never reached.

You flood my mind like the ocean tide

Slowly drifting out

Then I hear one song

Reminding me of you

And your waves come crashing down

Drowning me all over again.

Can you touch my soul the way you touch my skin?

Pluck my brows

Line my eyes

Pinch my cheeks

Paint my lips

All to look cute for you.

But now I choose me.

No longer do I push up my breasts

Shave daily

Paint my face

And now I feel more beautiful

For me.

No longer held back by your hate

Your words do echo in my head

My heart knew you weren't my soulmate

I feel alive even though our love is dead

I didn't expect this day to come

Where I would be the one who is strong

My body doesn't feel cold and numb

Freedom overcomes me knowing you were wrong

Taking all I had to walk away

Finally putting myself first

I have found my self-love and she is here to stay

All my love and passion is ready to burst

You taught me in the worst way

But my happiness is here to stay.

Despite all she has been through

Despite all the darkness

She still believes in magic

And true love.

She still believes in the good.

No matter how deep you have cut her

Her wounds will heal.

She herself is a unicorn.

It is okay to let the tears fall.

Have you ever seen how beautiful

The trees look after it rains?

The way the sun kisses my skin
Reminds me of your lips.
Making me want to hide away
From my favorite thing.
Until one day I stepped outside.
Feeling the warmth upon my shoulders
And my cheeks.
Bliss sending chill through my body
Making my skin tingle.
No longer does it hurt.
Now it reminds me of a happy time
When I was loved.

-healing

She has a mind like Wonderland.

Twisted

Curious

Sending her falling down the rabbit hole

But only she can

Can find her way out.

No white rabbit to lead her.

Everyone tells you to find someone to marry
and have a life with

But no one tells you it is okay to be alone.

She doesn't come around as often anymore.

The girl at the bar.

From time to time she is at the bar

Dancing alone.

Seducing those around her

With her hips.

That girl is poison

I guess that's why they call her

Suicide.

Love likes to hide in many places.

She knows every nook and cranny.

The places you never think to look.

Love is even easy to find

If you just open your eyes

And your heart to what is around you.

She will grace you with her presence

If you just let her in.

Let her embrace you.

Allow her to show you happiness.

Let her out of hiding.

His lips tasted like the end of the world and I was the only survivor.

If you look in the mirror and you don't like what you see

First clean it off

If that doesn't work

Go buy a new mirror.

Have you ever noticed how hard it is to capture a sunsets beauty in a photo?

You can use a filter or take 10 different photos

But it never quite captures the true beauty.

Remember that the next time your phone doesn't

Capture your essence in a selfie.

I was fine being alone.

I loved it.

Not worrying about anyone but me.

But then there you were.

Not looking for anything serious.

Still licking my wounds from the last one.

But you made me feel again.

No matter how tight I held onto my heart

You stole it from my bare hands.

Slowly I fell madly in love with you.

And there we were.

Until my heart grew too heavy for you to carry.

You dropped it.

Leaving me lost and empty.

I didn't understand.

My body ached for you.

But then I realized

You were put in my life to show me

How to feel again

And most importantly how to love again.

Secluding yourself to gain control of your mental health is not selfish.

Helping yourself is brave and courageous.

Some people do not have that kind of strength.

But you do.

And that's beautiful.

Buy the candy. Date the guy. Say yes to things you want. Say no to the things you don't. Take a leap. Read the book. Laugh loudly. Cry. Throw something against the wall. Jump on your bed. Dance to your favorite song. Sing the words at the top of your lungs. Smile at a stranger. Have sex. Sleep in. Drink tea. Take a shot of tequila. Laugh at yourself. Just please don't forget to have fun and love what you are doing. Your happiness is most important.

Some see the world in darkness.

But not her.

She searches for every crack of light

Planting flowers for hope to grow wild.

Her eyes held many moons and many stars

Her heart held the sun

Her ears are graced with silence

She is her own galaxy

And she is a Wanderess.

The problem was she always expected you to leave

 because that's what people always do

But you stayed and she liked it.

Until you overstayed your welcome.

Your silence was louder than all the speakers you played your shitty music through.

Dance like no one is watching even if everyone has their eyes on you.

Sometimes I lay here

Thinking about you

Wondering if you are

Thinking of me too.

Do you check up on me

The way I check up on you?

Do you stare at your door just hoping

I may walk through?

Have you deleted every

Trace of me from your phone?

Sometimes I lay here

Wondering if you are

Thinking of me too.

You taught me how I should be loved.

Making me feel my voice mattered.

Understanding my past cut me deeper

Than the ocean floors

But you made me feel I was more.

That didn't stop you from

Filling your loneliness

With someone else

Because the distance

Was too much for you to handle.

-I'm sorry you felt alone.

No man will ever make me feel lower than the ground I walk on ever again

They will be lucky if they can even reach the clouds I rest on.

Cry.

Yell.

Scream.

Dance it out.

Don't forget to feel

Every ounce of the pain.

Smile.

Laugh.

Dance freely

Knowing you made it

Through the darkness.

Nobody has ever seen something like you.

Keep that person safe at all costs.

Because they carried you to where you are now.

The light that you shine.

The energy you generate.

Nobody has ever seen something like you.

Her eyes shine like the sun

Energy pours out of her smile

She is love.

But she does not want to share

Her love with anyone

Except herself.

For her love runs deeper

Than time itself.

She believes no one is worthy.

No one has the kind of strength

To carry the weight of her affection.

Time wasted on waiting

For you to come around.

Maybe you wouldn't break this promise.

Maybe you changed in 22 years.

But I have grown tired of waiting

On broken clocks.

As I lay in bed alone I miss the way you used to touch me.

Sitting so close our legs would touch

Or our shoulders would brush.

Even as we sleep your hand would find mine

And I would wake up intertwined.

But my favorite way you touched me

Was when you spoke.

Your words fill the air with your passion

The deep vibrations of your voice wrapping around me

Pulling me in.

Your energy touched me so deeply I could feel your love

Even across the miles between us.

You started touching me less.

Sitting further away from me.

I noticed all of it as much as I tried to ignore it.

Then it was all over

And your touch was gone.

You taught me to open my gates again

No matter how dark and twisted one

May find what hides behind

One will come

To see only beauty.

Her beauty radiates from her core

Pulling everyone into her orbit.

She is love.

Captivating.

Enticing.

Her eyes shine like the northern lights

So incredibly beautiful you don't dare look away.

She is Beauty.

And a laugh so contagious

She could pull you out of your

Deepest sorrows.

She is everything good in the world

And more.

I see her confidence when she tries on a new dress

As her hands slide down her hips feeling her curves

Looking sexy as hell.

Watching her for years

Growing into a beautiful young woman.

I have seen her pain

Questioning herself.

Playing with new makeup styles because she thinks she needs it

She doesn't.

She talks to me sometimes

I am always listening.

For I am in love with her

The girl in the mirror.

There are times when I want to reach out and send you a text.

But people also think heroin is a good idea.

Cupids arrow has shot me in the ass too many times.

Can he find someone else to aim at?

He must find pleasure in making me fall madly in love then watching it crumble.

But maybe that's his point.

Making me fall in love even when I don't want to

Just to prove that I can.

Burying my emptiness only made room

For hate

For sadness

For regret

For resentment

Learning to push through made room

For love

For light

For smiles

For laughter

For joy

For new beginnings

You cannot hide from the pain or push it away.

Pain and emptiness wraps around your limbs like ivy

Until you take care of the problem and kill the weeds.

Forgiving those who have wronged you is a big step in healing and moving forward.

                        Especially when they don't deserve it.

But you do. You deserve to move forward.

                        Forgive those who don't deserve it

 for you.

Do it for YOU.

Falling in love take your breath away.

Making your stomach falling to your butt

Your heart race faster than a hummingbird's wings.

Falling in love is the most beautiful experience.

But falling out of love hurts like hell.

Hitting every branch on the way down from the high.

Laying on the ground covered in bruises.

Aching from the pain we are paralyzed.

Unsure of what to do next.

Do I lay here and suffer through the pain

Or do I get up?

Twists and turns will curl into your path at unexpected times

Just when you think you couldn't be any happier

A new branch will pop up

Tripping you

Sending your body falling to the ground.

When you finally get back onto your feet

Déjà vu

Back to the ground you go.

Eventually you build strength and calluses

You watch your footing.

The way you get back up and stay head strong is what

Will help you get through tomorrow.

Breath tastes like whiskey.
I got drunk from your lips.
Couldn't get enough
Until I became an alcoholic.

After you I searched for the buzz
his lips taste like vodka
and I fucking hate vodka.

Alcohol doesn't taste the same
To me anymore.
I can barely stomach the flavor
Let alone the aroma

That was until he told me my lips
Taste like tequila
And I love tequila.

Being desired by people is addicting.

The way they look but cannot touch

Or the way they touch but cannot have you.

Their words make you feel like a goddess

Like they see the same you that you see.

But when you finally let someone have every piece

Of your tender soul and

They abusive the gift you have given them,

It was not you who wasn't enough

It was they who could not bear the immensity

Of your beauty and love.

-you are still a goddess without him.

What is the point of you hiding away in my dreams

If you are not there when I need you when I'm conscious?

You will not find peace between my legs.

You can't fuck away your problems

Wear the dress that makes your curves pop.

Show off your long beautiful legs.

Let others see your beauty the way you see it.

Walk with confidence

Make your fire resilient.

Then no one can put you out.

Sometimes I look down at my wrists
And wonder about the girl at the bar.
How she looks dress in red.
If I spend a night with her will she stay forever
Or if she will only stay for the night.

You may have seen my body naked

But you will be lucky if I let you see

My naked soul.

                              First, I asked myself

When will I find someone who won't use me?

                              But I should've asked myself

When am I going to let people stop using me?

And to the women who have been told

they are not good enough by a man

You are good enough

So enough it scares him

Because he knows he isn't.

Once upon a time

I was your little mouse

Following at your feet wherever you went

Worshipping the ground you walked on.

You shrunk me down

Smaller

And smaller

Until you forgot about me

I built myself back up

Alone

Then you Noticed the beautiful tigress I became.

But it was too late

I loved me more than you ever could.

I became the queen of this jungle.

You were blind when I cried

You turned your back when I hurt

You were deaf when I spoke

You didn't like it when the roles reversed.

From a tiny seed, you grew me

Already have done this before

Adding another scared you.

Questioning your own strength.

Then came along your little girl.

Her big blue eyes looked at you like you held the moon

And all the stars.

You held her close and raised her tough.

With the tsunami of life coming at her

You kept her safe.

Building her to be strong and tough.

Watching her grow into a woman

Sturdy enough to take on her own tsunamis.

You are the strongest woman

And to her you still hold all the stars

and the moon.

-thank you momma

She is the light on a dark day

The first flowers of spring

The first cup of coffee in the morning

Laughter in the air

She is the moment

You look forward to each day

Open your eyes and find her.

She is everywhere.

He was the caffeine running through my veins

Sprouting energy from my core

Unable to get enough

But he was also the crash right after.

Trust was shattered by my own two hands

I bought all the duct tape and glue I could find

To fix it.

Piecing the Trust back together

Piece by piece.

Taking my time.

Giving everything, I had to fix what I broke.

And you let me believe I had

But you lied.

There was no forgiveness.

In just a blink of an eye

We didn't even give the glue

A chance to dry.

"Yes, there is someone else."

I didn't feel anger

Not even sadness.

All I felt was hurt.

you said you couldn't trust me

but in the end, it was I

who could not trust you.

Happiness will come and go

Because happiness is a feeling

Not a destination.

To my Airman-

Little bird

You are growing so fast

Always there when I need you

As I am for you.

You made the choice to leave the nest

To spread your wings.

Though I could not be more proud

I can't help but feel scared.

You have been by my side for most of my life

And I don't know what to do

When I can't protect you.

You are doing this for you

To protect us all.

Not down the street anymore

But in a whole different country

Spreading your wings for us.

Pushing to be your best.

I couldn't be prouder of you Little bird.

My heart is my bedroom

Messy.

Cluttered.

I distract myself

So I don't have to clean it.

Do memories hit you like a tidal wave?

One second you are enjoying the view of the beach

Every tree

All the people soaking up the sun's rays

The sound of the water

But then a memory of them comes crashing down on top of you

Drowning you

Can't find your way to the surface

Which way is up

Lost completely in the ocean of them

Forgetting how to swim

How to breathe

Until finally

You break the surface

And your lungs fill with air.

Go ahead and hurt me.

Honey, I'll just turn you into poetry.

-*Bibbidi Bobbidi Boo*

Please don't kill yourself today.

Not today because you still have 3 more seasons on your favorite show.

Please don't kill yourself today

Because your brothers would miss you

And your momma would break.

Please don't kill yourself today

Not today because you just bought new shampoo

Or tomorrow because you have leftovers in the fridge.

Please don't kill yourself today

Because you already paid this month's rent

Please don't kill yourself today

This is the sign you asked the sky for

Please don't kill yourself today

Because I am asking nicely

And you have so many more tears to shed

Many more smiles to feel.

Please don't kill yourself today.

"This doesn't feel real" she said.

But it was.

Watching the doctor turn off the life support

To her best friend.

Silence.

Her last breath falls from her lips.

Gone.

"but I just talked to her" she said.

Flatline.

Stillness.

"It doesn't look like her" she said.

Because it wasn't.

She is gone.

You are holding me but I am not close enough

    My bare skin is touching yours but I am not close enough.

I lay on top of you naked feeling your heartbeat next to mine

    But I am not close enough.

You are inside me but I am not close enough.

    Goodbye kiss

And I knew I could never get close enough.

Tongue like a razor blade

Slicing and cutting

With my words not caring

who suffered massive blood loss.

He changed like the seasons.

Always changing

Unsure of who to be

Wanting to be warm like Summer

His mind stays in the chill of Winter.

There we the in between moments too

Like Spring and the Fall

Where he was happy.

Close to being where he wanted

Feeling how he wanted

But he believed the Groundhog

And let Winter stay

Longer than needed.

I was the sunrise and the sunset all in one

But you were looking at your phone.

The bees start swarming

First one

Then another

Ten. Twenty.

Swarming with questions

Doubts

More questions and doubts

Buzzing around my brain like bees

Buzzing so loud I cannot

Hear my own thoughts.

The bees make their nest in my brain

Taking over.

My body begins to buzz

As the anxiety bees

Take over.

You were the missing piece of the puzzle.

Edges and curves fit so perfectly

Then you tried to change your shape

And you didn't fit anymore.

Completely changing the puzzle.

Throwing blame around like darts

But never pinning one on yourself

Sticking everyone else with your pain

Never feeling the pain, yourself.

Everyone hiding their voices

Too afraid to throw the darts

Back at you.

Until finally one stepped up.

Causing your anger to run and hide

As the darts came flying back in your direction.

You are not dead but you still haunt me.

I hear your footsteps and your voice

Feeling your hands touching my body

Watching over my shoulder

Always there

Stealing every breath that enters my lungs

Lurking in my dreams.

Whispering your harassing words

Shouting at my imperfections.

You are not dead but you still haunt me.

Today you took a piece of me.

Yesterday is was two

Next week it will be 5.

No.

I will not allow it.

Today I am taking those pieces back

Putting myself back together.

Buzzing. Buzzing. Buzzing. Buzzing. Buzzing.
Buzzing. Buzzing. Buzzing. Buzzing. Buzzing.
Buzzing. Buzzing. Buzzing. Buzzing. Buzzing.
Buzzing. Buzzing. Buzzing. Buzzing. Buzzing.
Buzzing. Buzzing. Buzzing. Buzzing.

Buzzing. Buzzing. Buzzing. Buzzing. Buzzing.
Buzzing. Buzzing. Buzzing. Buzzing. Buzzing.
Buzzing. Buzzing. Buzzing. Buzzing. Buzzing.
Buzzing. Buzzing. Buzzing. Buzzing. Buzzing.
Buzzing. Buzzing. Buzzing. Buzzing.

Buzzing. Buzzing. Buzzing. Buzzing. Buzzing.
Buzzing. Buzzing. Buzzing. Buzzing. Buzzing.
Buzzing. Buzzing. Buzzing. Buzzing. Buzzing.
Buzzing. Buzzing. Buzzing. Buzzing. Buzzing.
Buzzing. Buzzing. Buzzing. Buzzing.

Buzzing. Buzzing. Buzzing. Buzzing. Buzzing.
Buzzing. Buzzing. Buzzing. Buzzing. Buzzing.
Buzzing. Buzzing. Buzzing. Buzzing. Buzzing.
Buzzing. Buzzing. Buzzing. Buzzing. Buzzing.
Buzzing. Buzzing. Buzzing. Buzzing.

Buzzing. Buzzing. Buzzing. Buzzing. Buzzing.
Buzzing. Buzzing. Buzzing. Buzzing. Buzzing.
Buzzing. Buzzing. Buzzing. Buzzing. Buzzing.
Buzzing. Buzzing. Buzzing. Buzzing. Buzzing.
Buzzing. Buzzing. Buzzing. Buzzing.

Buzzing. Buzzing. Buzzing. Buzzing. Buzzing.
Buzzing. Buzzing. Buzzing. Buzzing. Buzzing.

Buzzing. Buzzing. Buzzing. Buzzing. Buzzing.
Buzzing. Buzzing. Buzzing. Buzzing. Buzzing.
Buzzing. Buzzing. Buzzing. Buzzing.

Buzzing. Buzzing. Buzzing. Buzzing. Buzzing.
Buzzing. Buzzing. Buzzing. Buzzing. Buzzing.
Buzzing. Buzzing. Buzzing. Buzzing. Buzzing.
Buzzing. Buzzing. Buzzing. Buzzing. Buzzing.
Buzzing. Buzzing. Buzzing. Buzzing.

Buzzing. Buzzing. Buzzing. Buzzing. Buzzing.
Buzzing. Buzzing. Buzzing. Buzzing. Buzzing.
Buzzing. Buzzing. Buzzing. Buzzing. Buzzing.
Buzzing. Buzzing. Buzzing. Buzzing. Buzzing.
Buzzing. Buzzing. Buzzing. Buzzing.

Buzzing. Buzzing. Buzzing. Buzzing. Buzzing.
Buzzing. Buzzing. Buzzing. Buzzing. Buzzing.
Buzzing. Buzzing. Buzzing. Buzzing. Buzzing.
Buzzing. Buzzing. Buzzing. Buzzing. Buzzing.
Buzzing. Buzzing. Buzzing. Buzzing.

Buzzing. Buzzing. Buzzing. Buzzing. Buzzing.
Buzzing. Buzzing. Buzzing. Buzzing. Buzzing.
Buzzing. Buzzing. Buzzing. Buzzing. Buzzing.
Buzzing. Buzzing. Buzzing. Buzzing. Buzzing.
Buzzing. Buzzing. Buzzing. Buzzing.

Buzzing. Buzzing. Buzzing. Buzzing. Buzzing.
Buzzing. Buzzing. Buzzing. Buzzing. Buzzing.
Buzzing. Buzzing. Buzzing. Buzzing. Buzzing.

Buzzing. Buzzing. Buzzing. Buzzing. Buzzing. Buzzing. Buzzing. Buzzing. Buzzing.

The Bees don't have a mute or pause button.
They come when they please.

And they don't leave.

She is the stillness in the morning

Before the rest of the world is awake

There she is.

Her quiet is soothing

While her silence is deadly.

The stars still twinkle in her eyes

Before the sun hits the horizon.

As the sun rises,

Glistening off her skin,

Her bright energy

Will embrace you with warmth.

Take every moment with her you can.

There will be a lot of starless nights

Without her.

You were my favorite song on a sunny day.

Every time the words play through my speakers

My body ignites with excitement

Taking over my thoughts

Spreading across my face.

Singing along word for word at the top of my lungs

With the windows down.

Hair blowing around in every direction

Tickling my neck like your kisses.

Every single minute I spent with you

Felt like I had that song on repeat.

Until you changed the words.

She was put into your life unexpectedly.

Those big blue eyes captured your heart.

You held her when she cried.

Made her laugh.

The first man she ever loved.

As she grew older together you grew closer.

Through those big blue eyes

She saw a hero.

Stronger than Superman

Tougher than Wolverine

Braver than Daredevil

You built her to be her own Wonder Woman.

No man will ever compare to you.

You were the man who stepped up and gave a shit

The one who showed her she was important

Showed her the way she deserves to be treated.

Today you are still her hero

Her world.

Fix your pain the way you want.

Sleep.

Eat what you want.

Paint.

Have sex with who you want.

Run.

Do what helps you heal.

You will get through it but on your own terms.

but do NOT hide from the pain.

Don't be the one who chases.

You are the tequila

Not the lime

Let them be salty baby.

I heard you still ask about me.

Checking up on me.

Seeing if I am doing better without you.

Well I am.

I am thriving without you, living my best life.

You showed me exactly how I don't want to be treated.

I hope it hurts like hell.

Living from your pain

Learned from your lies

Grew from the struggle.

Beauty is in the eye of the beholder

Be your own beholder

Because you are beautiful

And that is amazing.

Her eyes pulled me in again.

Buzz.

Couldn't get her out of my head.

Buzz. Buzz.

She kept calling my name.

Buzz.

Reaching out for my hand.

Buzz. Buzz.

Pulling me closer to her.

Buzz.

The anxiety bees are flying toward the girl from the bar

Like she an intoxicating flower.

Buzz. Buzz.

We were the outsiders.

You and I.

They didn't see it that way.

We were half-bloods.

You were my big brother

And I was just your quiet kid sister.

Protecting me from the monsters

Of our world.

Fighting your own demons

While you saved me from mine.

"There you are. Your sparkle is shiny bright again." She said.

-I found us. I found me.

You warned me.

Had a bright flashing sign

Telling me not to.

But I was drawn to the light

While you were sitting in the dark.

Another shot.

Stinging all the way down.

Drunk kisses.

Shot.

Never dancing alone.

Teasing.

Shot.

Always goes home alone.

Leaving them wanting

Like you did to me.

Two months spent sleep walking.

Wondering around lost.

Stranded in the lifeless talking.

Begging to get out no matter the cost.

Sleep paralysis taking over

Unable to wake

Worse than a hangover

Anxiously waiting for a break.

I held you once.

In my dreams.

You smiled up to me

With those big blue eyes.

A smile spread across your cheeks

While my heart ached.

Never wanting to wake up

Wanting to watch you grow up.

Hoping you stay in my arms forever.

But I woke up

You were gone.

You didn't know that when you called me fat I already knew.

My body dysmorphic disorder shouts in my ear every time I look in the mirror or want to buy the beautiful tight dress.

You didn't know when you called me a bitch or told me I cry too much that I had already slept with the girl from the bar.

Before you. Before us. I found her. And she held me in the darkness but did not want me.

Your words sliced deeper than any blade but you didn't know because you didn't care.

You wanted to cut me open.

Wanted to shoot me down with every bullet you carried.

When I realized your insecurities couldn't bruise me anymore.

I became bulletproof

While you stay licking your wounds.

Love is so intriguing.

He is the handsome man you run into at the store

She is the gorgeous woman that made your coffee.

He is the adorable puppy at the park

She is the intoxicating smell of flowers.

But when you find her after she has been hiding

    Don't be scared.

Thou were a prince in my eye

But through your own you were no greater than a peasant

Never looking ahead.

Even Fairy Godmother herself could see your destiny.

Evil sorcerers took control over your mind

Making you make look like the fool.

Little did you know I am the Queen

And you could have been my King.

Now who is the fool?

Our bodies are our temples

Very own galaxy

No one gets to dictate what happens to our worlds

But ourselves.

Don't let your voice get lost in space.

Pain does not hide here anymore.

Sometimes he comes to visit but I refuse to open the door.

Using his candied words to sweeten me up

But I will no longer drink from that cup.

Worrying about the past will not heal

Allow the cuts to heal

Some may turn to scars

While others will soon be forgotten.

"You have amazing eyes."

"Your body is so sexy."

"Perfect little pouty lips."

"Long sexy legs for days."

"That ass is out of this world."

"You're so beautiful."

Don't compliment my appearance in hopes of winning my heart.

Compliment my brain and my mind and you will win my soul.

Seeing you for the first time since you broke my heart

Didn't hurt as bad as I thought.

Then you hugged me

Turning me into a puddle

Wanting to melt into your arms all over again

But I was strong and pulled away

No matter how badly I wanted to stay.

As hard as I try I cannot wash my hands of you

Scrubbing like a surgeon before surgery

But your germs are glued to me

Infecting everyone I touch.

No one wants to come near me

With fear of infection.

Waiting for a cure

Or maybe someone who is immune

To your bullshit.

Our first kiss got me drunk

The second made me an alcoholic.

All the best parts of me are hidden.

They are not hard to get to if you start digging.

This is no Wonderland

Certainly not Narnia

Positive we aren't in Kansas anymore

We are entirely bonkers

Let us get lost in a world of our own.

She may seem to be strong because she never cries.

Her emotions remain guarded.

Those who have seen her sadness remain haunted.

Seeing her in their dreams

Wishing they had not done her wrong.

Trying everything to rid their minds of her

But she remains a ghost.

The pain may feel too much to carry

Feeling as though it may never end

Breathe.

Take a breath.

Lighten your load.

One day soon you will wake up

To find the pain is gone

And you have made it.

Be darkness

Be light

Just don't hide in the shadows anymore.

I should have left when you didn't tell me you love me.

I should have left when you cheated on our anniversary.

I should have left when your mom told me to.

I should have left when you stopped touching me.

I should have left when you touched me in a way I did not want.

I should have left when you expected me to be someone I am not.

I should have left when you screamed in my face.

I should have left when you always missed my birthday.

I should have left when you read my journal.

I should have left when you told me I cry too much.

I should have left when your videogames came first.

I should have left when you left me all alone when I needed you most.

I should have left when you said you didn't like my family.

I should have left when you didn't choose me.

I put up with you for too long and you knew that.

And I left.

Now you regret all the things you did and want me back

But only because you see that I am happy without you.

You miss seeing me happy

Ironically, I'm always happy when you are not here.

We stay in hopes they will become the person we want them to be

Or we stay waiting for the person we fell in love with comes back.

Focusing all our energy on them

We lose sight of ourselves.

Don't lose you in the process of

waiting for someone else.

When the tequila takes over

My inner bitch comes out to play

She's a hunter

On the prowl

In search for her next victim.

Her eyes shine brighter than the stars in the sky

While her smile illuminates the day

She is light.

-she found her sparkle

Be your own kind of beautiful.

Don't listen to the girl from the bar.

She lies.

Thought breaking my bed would make me want to stay

That was your problem.

Thinking with your dick

Made you a dick.

You lost sight of my worth

But I didn't.

Now I glow

While you sulk in the shadows.

You only miss me when you are drunk

Called me when you were sober to say sorry

Always falling for your tricks

Growing angrier with myself

For being blinded by love

Our love was a one-way street

Now the road is closed

Never to reopen.

Trying your best to find shortcuts

Little do you know the destination has changed

Gone without a trace.

Blocked.

Cannot write

Cannot call.

Once I realized my worth

I was too expensive for you to afford.

Your touch triggered a fire inside

I had forgot existed

Remaining guarded

For I do not trust many

But your deep blue eyes

Pull me in like the tide

Pushing my heart in two different directions

Wanting nothing more to allow myself to fall

Deeper

And deeper

Into your ocean

The lifeguard remains on duty

Just in case you leave me drowning

In your wake

Fear climbs inside my body when someone threatens to take my heart

Whispering lies to my mind

Making her overthink

Building the walls before you even

Have a chance to catch a glimpse

Of my captivating heart.

My heart has been ripped from my chest without warning

Left unprotected

Stolen

But this time I don't think I want it back.

Are you the one who can save me

From this dreadful tower?

Your smile is pure seduction

But it wasn't until I kissed

The lips of Temptation himself

I knew I was in deep trouble.

She is falling

Further. Deeper.

Doesn't think you will catch her

Those before enjoyed seeing her pain

Watching her suffer from the heartache.

Who is to say you are not the same?

Do you see in me what I see?

Now look with your heart.

What do you see?

One of the bravest things you will ever do

Is love again.

Allow love in

Let her take over

Feel her embrace

Her warmth.

Don't fear her.

You are the song I cannot get out of my head

Playing on repeat

As I hum along to the melody

Never growing tired of you

I ask only one thing

Please don't change the words on me.

His words should never poison your soil

Baby girl you are a beautiful flower

Find someone who knows how to nourish

Helping you bloom.

When you are alone

Don't forget to water

Show yourself some Love.

Care for your soil.

You tell me to make a wish everyday

Before you I made many wishes

A wish for laughter

A wish for a prince

A wish to be saved

A wish to be loved

A wish for a best friend

Some went to waste

Losing my faith in the wishes

For they never came true

Days

Months

Years

But then there they were

Slowly coming true

Little did I know

I was wishing for you.

-11:11

Boys were all poison

Infecting my brain

Wreaking my heart

Frying my immune system

Until I found my cure

Healing me in ways

I didn't know I needed

Making me strong

Stronger than before.

You are worth every mile

Between us

Two hours and forty-nine minutes

One hundred and eighty miles

I would drive them every single day

Just to spend an hour with you

Time stops

The second our eyes lock

Unsure which way is up

Trapped in a trance

I never want to leave.

Lightening.

Flashing across the sky

Only few are lucky to capture

A bolt in a photo

But somehow, I am your photographer

You are my lightening.

Together

A work of art.

Your arms wrap around my body like ivy

Holding me in a way I have never felt before

Your vines keeping me close to you

Warming my skin

Through to my heart

The grip remains tight

As I rest my head upon your chest

Allowing your embrace to take control.

Love is no longer the queen hide and seek

She can only hide for so long

I found her in a place I never would never guessed

The same place the dangerous beautiful girl dances

I didn't give up

I couldn't give up

Knowing she was still out there waiting for me

Love distracts me from her

Making me forget all about her

Leading me onto the right path

Showing me what truly matters

Her.

With you I don't hear the bees

The girl from the bar doesn't come around

You make me feel human

There is no pattern

We are not robots

Sucked into doing what everyone else wants to see.

Living in a world of our own

With you my mind is free to be.

-I hope the girl from the bar gets stung by the bees

The girl in the mirror finally sees her true beauty.

I dumped the girl at the bar.

Love stopped playing hide and seek

The bees don't buzz as often

I rid myself of you

Your voice no longer echoes in my head

But the journey does not end here

Not even close.

How is it I let myself fall so hard so fast?

Never meaning to

My heart just flew out of my chest

Into your hands

As if it were never mine in the first place.

I try to hide my feelings for as long as possible

Not wanting to scare you away

Unable to help myself

Trapped in my own emotions.

-yours

I am the Coke

You are the Mentos.

Showing me love like no one before

You dove right in

Making my heart bubble with emotion

Unable to screw the cap on quick enough

After letting you in

All of my love rushing to get out

Exploding everywhere

Covering all surfaces around us

Out in the open

No longer hiding in the bottle

Here I stand with my love pouring out

Scared for you to notice

All so new

So fresh

Didn't think I could feel this deeply

This quickly

But there you were.

Both were bruised

Unsure of what you wanted

But then you kissed me

Under the blue and purple lights

Tequila on my lips

Your hands holding my face

My heart opened to you with a kiss

You stole it completely

When you bought me shampoo

Each time you steal kisses at red lights

When your hand rests on my thigh

The little kisses upon my cheek

While I shift in my sleep

The way you hold me close.

Somehow making me feel like I am

The only girl in the world.

Now the bruises are fading

And I know what I want.

Acknowledgments

My Rae of sunshine, who pushed me to write this. No matter how dark and twisted it became.

Dad, who without knowing, showed me poetry is a form of healing. You are my rock. My safety net when the bees come.

My family, the crazy bunch who help me ignore the girl from the bar. I don't know what I would do without every single one of you. Made of strong women and amazing men who all support the millions of different paths I take, guiding me with their own experiences.

Friends, the creative little beings who show me what warmth feels like in the winter. Each one brings different light into my life helping me shine my brightest.

My love, who shows me how to truly be loved and supports my writing (even though I never let him read it). When you came into my life I thought I had finished my book but the more time I spent with you the more writing I needed to get out. You inspired me to change my ending.

I love you all.

Made in the USA
San Bernardino, CA
10 August 2018